a women

KUHL HOUSE POETS
edited by Mark Levine and Emily Wilson

a women
by vanessa roveto

University of Iowa Press, Iowa City

University of Iowa Press, Iowa City 52242
Copyright © 2020 by Vanessa Roveto
www.uipress.uiowa.edu
PRINTED IN THE UNITED STATES OF AMERICA

Design by Kristina Kachele Design, llc

Printed on acid-free paper

Library of Congress Cataloging-in-Publication Data
Name: Roveto, Vanessa, author.
Title: a women / Vanessa Roveto.
Description: Iowa City : University of Iowa Press, [2020] |
Series: Kuhl House Poets
Identifiers: LCCN 2020006510 (print) | LCCN 2020006511
(ebook) | ISBN 9781609387341 (paperback) |
ISBN 9781609387358 (ebook)
Subjects: LCGFT: Poetry.
Classification: LCC PS3618.O87253 W66 2020 (print) |
LCC PS3618.O87253 (ebook) | DDC 811/.6—dc23
LC record available at https://lccn.loc.gov/2020006510
LC ebook record available at https://lccn.loc.gov/2020006511

for relationship

Parts One

When we first met, we shared the same vanishing point emptiness
that needed to settle. The small European country she came
from ventilated longing, measuring its austerity against history.
I remember a world contracting with each utterance, a steadily
expanding vertigo of zooming in and out on an object becoming a
subject. I may have loved her from the beginning, knowing it would
end for that reason

....

.....
....

....

....

....

....

....

....

At the event, the woman she was tailing was small-big. We were all mourning privately the death of the unisex sweater, the gender-belligerent frame. Her mood matched tender tastes made more enjoyable through Ray-Bans. The fake succulent made a connection between nature outside and in her, a very ancient form of space dressing, purity of making it raw. The beating of artificial inspirations were played to match a rhythm. The womans purse went to the bathroom, summer sticking hardest in downtown, like Cold War milk, like the skin exterior of a virgin 60s style all the way up to the refrigerated 90s. She asked for the womans cells, numbers

....

....

.....

....

....

....

....

....

....

..

. . ..

.   ...

The parked Toyota fucked us near Astro Diner that fist date. One
of us said *thank u*, but we both felt it. It's a scare that a relationship
begins in medias res, as if it had always existed, screaming itself. A
prehistory concurrent with the present tense zombie. There was the
future as well, the erotic possibility in the fullness of lips, creeping
fingers over a horizon. The cliché that desire dilated the universe
was our out-of-body parallel. What happened to her belonged to
her. No memory of fertility in the low-lit hatchback. A steamy nipple
session beyond laboring animal skins. Roughed-up silence a lust-
filled contract

....

....   /

....

....

....

/ /

.... /

....

Her letter became a ladder, an amateur honeypot to the sky. Sting-
ing became the verb for a swollen blood clot that stifled the nerves,
connecting eternity to the point where spandex dissolved. The
clouds revolved around their intimate spaces. The seatbelt was a
restraint pump, ready. The loose ponytail lost its cinch to make way
for a tight ass leaving planet earth

.... ///////

......

. ...

... ...

....

//////////////////////   ////////////////

At the Silverlake dogs park, my sameness had a crush on her, how
clean I keep up my skinned quotient, the right amount of sister
in any recipe. She left no child behind. Her words were nameless
unspoken low-key boredom, a thicket of glass nesting in eggs.
Courting slivers on the playing ground, my connection with her
was a way of reproducing second nature the way capitalism watches
and feels. Her womens mother replayed the horror film scene that
took place in a shared commune as a feeling not an identity. A
picnic basket filled itself with dirt, the reparative potential of a little
death on the screen side of things. Instead of just levitating, they
levitated

/////
    /////

//////////////////////

//

////////////////////////

///////// //////////////

.. ....

She was over the pain of dancing with myself at Akbar, not her actual sunset just a different rise. They choked on each others in a hard-work way. She thought a woman who doesn't wear perfume has no future. God was dead, inevitable. She obeyed the acts of feminism on a boy body for fair market price. The gin tonic slid into a slimy booth as peanuts cracked their shells. Choking on shards, she stopped editing. We both bought tickets to the sky, or thought they did

...... /./././/

////////////////////////

/ / /   /////////

The case of the bold brunette with the denim jacket tied to her neck:
A sight that spent beyond. She was differently the same girl smell, a
side effect self-portrait in search of Arthur. Everyones drunk ideas
had become the raw stuff casting into the net. To survive romantic
love, the woman served the other woman desert dirt with shells as
the truck stop receded into the distance. The barnacles were man-
acles. She gathered the polyester sheets because they were loaded
guns in leopard print. The bed poured pyramids of Salton Sea atop
their limbs until sleep turned them into hard matters. The body
glove was full. She remembered nothing of the past ripple effect of
leather skin, of tits so expensive they came of age in stones. With
each new mom element, the yellowed mattress couldn't tell the
difference between its worn springs or its splintered past. Our safe
word was dental floss. Say I love you we said I love you they said

.....

///

                                                              .....

/////////////////

. ...

The love must be real because to know a place she hates. It was an
underbelly education, a coffee space reformatted Korean church
downtown, no public hairs allowing the crossing of golden turmeric
latte. Palms fed sweat moving in together the way fear felt guilt. The
womans desire was mistranslated and flat-footed as the froth came
in her ear. She had no monopoly on grief. The two women smiled
but only one C cup was upright milked erect. Yearned intimacy
was hysterical because even the air cries a loose valve in bad water
pressure

. . .
////

..

The Valley girl rendezvoused with the xs european at the public
water fountain stretched tightly under the acid-washed landscape.
In the murky reflection, they mirrored scissored and sistered over
the piece of spit at the corner. Trees were an afterthought carried
by the wind up her nostrils. All orifices were one, like every film
in which Charlotte Gainsbourg is an impression of herself doing
herself. There's a castration scene to make the chapped extra
felt. Skinny jeans cotton conflating all over the seams with sad
ejaculation. The sappy bark peeled itself off

..

/../../../../..

/

One night she threads me out and tells me someone knew something they can't know someone knew something she didn't. She tells me to move my chair away from her wall. Now she pulls a soft punch and a street clamp. One of us decides to play tag, not knowing exactly what that means. Blind metaphors sought revenge for sloppy leftovers. She ate the wheat grass in one gulp

/

. . . .

. .

.

.

At the full Monty bar, she answered herself to the bartender.
The woman greeted her stool with laws of lechery, an outbreak of
fingers moving the wood closer, like a mothers neverending per-
sona coming and going. Logorrhea had been marked by the white
coat as a classic symptom of marketplace trauma, a douchebags
conflation. The ginger beer took a deep breath and made a decision
to up its content. The bartender said the mint muddler was the per-
sonification of her boyfriends ripped penis the night the sublunary
met the hallucinatory. She wanted her to beg for chews, nutting
into her flattened ear. The sticky red booth sunk lower. Vocab was
bludgeoned

. . . .

. .

.

.

. . . .

. ... .

. .

.

.

She wrote the other woman screenplays, poems, text after text,
longing growing longer. She made her an audio file, named a sand-
wich after her nose and sent five pictures of handsome captures.
The lone animal yearned in a Los Angeles zoo. The caged descrip-
tion of the creatures alignment was attuned to the magic weapon
of intermittent reinforcement. Everyone had been impressed with a
wet enclosure. A barely there thong slipped to one side for the show.
The furred touch started an altar light. She agreed to teach me mas-
tering, to alter language, and i became small, her

///////

..... .

. . . .

. ... .

. .

.

I boarded her runaway plane. It was the last of my money, that silver bondage, and I wanted to enslave myself to someone. Me she we, it wasn't a choice of matter. We were connected by tax breaks and airborne bag nausea. The film playing on the plastic tray messaged me *shhh don't tell anyone what goes on in this apartment complex.* The stale croissant suffocated under its plastic as the childs spork went numb. The woman had been reduced to snack size, the crunch and crush of ego death, appealing only to laymen. Under the limpidity of her anemic angel hair, she had creeping grief headspots. Whether she liked it or not in this dead corpse water, ruins ruined themselves, weird notes of graffiti rewriting the wrong side of a pillar 'your body my rules'

./././

In their meat place she was counterfeit. They tested chicken breasts
against blood to make glucose rise to the occasion of the miracle
turning muscle to milk. The paper napkins un-plyed themselves,
along with pity, the womans hand reaching toward a past. There
was excitability between stereo speakers in the old world of mono
nostalgia. The context was no contest. The repertory of disorders
was a slipper slope conducive to her sliding scale of authoritarian
girl violence. The city experienced its own dog desire for ownership,
for forgotten leash loneliness. I begged her to braid my bush, pony-
tail it, dye it pink or remove it from hell

/ / / /

...

The passions of European suicides increased with the small-plate assumption that tapas never suffer. Epic exposure to the elements was a sign of independence. The worn idealistic tapestry of an internal law, the culpability of the wild west. At night, the Mediterranean windows closed by themselves as the curtains tried to find metaphors to exert control over the heat. Seaweed slicked into the room though the coast was away for the winter. A measure of red wine bled from the tender scroll. She was deaf and mute when they said we wanted her to know we aren't there. The sprinkler system had been shut off, all the tobacco had been smoked, the American flag could no longer be humped

....

....

....

....

/ ///////////

....

Back home, she grabs the Blame Dildo, stiffening up the upper
lip. At night, she begins taking vaginal authority to the next level,
crying while masterbaiting, taking her back to Naomi Watts Towers
to the history of LA barbed-wire camp. Piping hot, no one can
understand her drug, nor the bug crawling out of the revolver. The
she-burn in place, sudden onset homelessness as mysterious as the
weight of her buzz-cut thigh. No one can remember how the eggs fit
neatly into trapped air. Every dilator opens the cosmos to a ceme-
tery dandelions avoid. Even the chickweed hates it

///
///
///
///............../////..........//////.............//////....
.........//////......//////

.

.

/

.   . . .

.

Enjoy the alone time she flayed. The leashed child got up and texted her
persona in person, stuck between being ones and being a checking
account without balance. I was picked on at space, my toes wedding to
cracked wood to break the fall. The younger athlete felt itchy, sub-
merged her thoughts in an ice bath, her mind creating dopamine jock
cream. A *Vogue* article read to itself. I couldn't recall the last time I
thought about No Pussy Season, no common surround sound. The bed
was a shed, intimacy a power tool to enter new furniture arrangements.
Minutes wore themselves on. The used pillows bled out

....

. . . .

. . .

After basic math, she calculated her losses and measured them
against the sum of weight gain. She had become fat soluble. Her
goddess cards arranged themselves at the table, the moment of
no self, no life goals, only snap-on judgment. A face was nothing
but a weird plastic mask on a death mask, facing outward the day
she was born. She reconstructed events to produce a new pretend
agency: Dumb techno beats downloaded into reduced gray matter.
Proletariat limbs were means not ends. Prayers were designed to
destroy Gap jeans, like a TV hooked into her for hump day. Toast
burnt itself into ashes

/
//
///

....
......
...
.

. . . .

. . .

/././

....

Two deer stood poised down in the San Fernando Valley as the
train passed by, like some odd-tasting tableau vivant in the Natural
History Museum, framed in the rectangular window heading
north heading south. Her mourning had become a forest, a desire
collage. Sounds entering from the walls, the halls, nut butter
traveling from online voices to the dim resident. The text message
read *sory* and turned itself over, sucking fingers for salted almond
kisses. The potent grip on thirst loosened like a hard stool at the
bar, 38-year-old mail sent to harass the woods, to bark up her mossy
tree. Her face against the coral-like patterns of the fungus, pinged
by pinecones

/././

....

..

.....

///////////////////////

... ...

At the mall, she was becoming intimate with an inept mannequin, pegging her salary offer to its fashion torso. Zombies eye-shopped and sifted together. Anger was measured and trayed by each food court stall, each redundant à la carte. She was no longer menu'd. The lukewarm hot dog slipped out of its stale pretzel across the embittered slab. The preparer caught it in her latex gloves to remind her she had a job to do. Across the way were end-of-life doughnuts. All the asses began to itch as denim sat moping in the chair, stuck crying over anothers leftover method. Some of the dust creatures hid in iced water, reduced to a monotone 'her'

//   //////////////////////////

/.///

No one could recognize Pale-Faced Traveler, neighborhood cats
clawing at her flaked walking lunch. As a discounted doormat, gay
blame became shame. Her clothing choice reduced to a single cross
body bag, her subjectivity a princess with alopecia, eating crabs she
gave herself. The neighbors continued to swarm voices like bees.
The birthday flowers wilted on purpose, petals dropping, pain the
earth feels when sneakered. It was the day the other woman moved
out, the day the mask bent downward, blending into a system of
safe belongings. Welcome

. . .

The person she was going to revisit was her first kiss in the mouth. Failing to understand the strokes, the stiff brushes, why the striped horse was sad and haunted by its bad haircut and purple bruises, the lie told her to feel entering into someone. The dog had died that year and it was a symbol of her faults. Her guilt ached in my spine, the scoliosis of Egon Schiele without worldwide fame, without the cult. That was the beautiful analogy she came on. The gallery held them both in a corner, and she squinted to make her small enough to pocket and protect. Commodity cultures fingers moved over pockets of cellulite. The curatorial statement erased itself. She me her I we them us

. .

. . . .

Doing bed labor, she couldn't get the story or the old pudding to set,
no matter how hard she fingered its center. The milky way was no
match for the spoon, which she took to her thinning thigh, remem-
bering the time she wanted to role-play with pasties, play dough to
her kneads. No saucy diplomacy, just organic matter in an ancient
lakebed. At that moment the woman would have reminded her of
her mother if only she could have let her, or left her. The expira-
tion date on her memory on a carousel. The playlist played its own
future

. . . .

. . . . . .

. . . .

. . . .

. . . .

.....

.....

.. . .

.. ..

/ / / / /

This new woman experienced an echo of naval homesickness, the dialogue repetition in a submarine movie. It was a reminder that the correlations between houseboat and self are always watercolored precarious. The electrical currents connecting to remind her, the archipelago networking people with civil defensiveness training. At the long pier she was always doing her best to sync with the person in front of her, to sew a steeple from the synaptic, the static, to turn scraps into scrapbooks, into book-books, into bookstores, into newsstands on a boardwalk filled with mementos, rusted tines of the fork

/ / / / /

..

... .

. . ..

In the feminine CVS aisle, grief signed off on being disproportion-
ate as downer pads spread wings. Her cheap blouse was the house
band of blues. Pantyliners commiserated about a desire for connec-
tion, for a more secure attachment. She saw her reflection in the
plastic coating crotch, in the history of womans suffering rendered
sticky pink. Sporty tubes shoved feeling into the painful parts. A
message over the counter ticked her earlobe into eyes. She had to
update her cells phone number. The discount registered the differ-
ence between sanity and sanitary. Four machine minutes later, the
coupon printed ribbons to enfold the lady napkins

. . . .

. . . .

..

...

....

She feels the sensate center moving again from the poverty of its original cause. There was an energy to the laziness of an updated wiki description of the *Baywatch* episode where the world ends. The brain goes where it knows, each abandoned floatie ballooning the history of an implanted memory syndrome. On the Santa Monica Pier, cream crackers exit an eyehole into an oyster. Drugged mushrooms are able to see the beautiful demented lunacy of surfboards. A mom striped bathing suit, convening with the muddy sand castles, the ocean bath, pieces of plastic, neon gems, dead skin, dead scrolls, scales balancing the weight of warmed blubber against the shore. An intricate timeliness, borne of fat, a turning away from bright lights. The final days were closing in, collapsing under the weight of norm porn. I hear her whisper. A word filled the carcass with cunts

Idlewild Retreat

1: a year late her she asks the image in the cracked
mirror what's life with an extra breast removed

a raw contusion. the enemy of an arm ending in a partially
severed hand. the bottom of the frame, the black of her cave,
a debasement, a poor and empty room furnished with a
simple iron rod. dead center, a forefinger lovely and mute,
supple, silent. light blacking-out her eye, the jagged line
between the others brown bangs, white forehead. browbeat
scar

suddenly turned back, caught in the glare of exhumation.
behind and to the left, in her portfolio, one arm outstretched
toward cadavertown, shadows moving across spectral time
zones. five thrusts: the corner of a sharpened wooden dress.
dust motes caught up in sudden light. a soiled seedbed and a
crouching figure, signaling up tawdry floorboards. the
lateral slit zipper

sex: a mouth and a mouth, gender neuter, a gentle
downward frowning. above their nose, twin orbs concentrate
obliterating light. tiny bubbles slowly rise to the surface.
around them, nothing

2: what's to love about mom is: mom

i spend words mentioning her to a mind reader i pay to hear
she is a feeling. a sequence of explosive acts. dimensionless.
a cosmic sentence filled with gender nouns. a grocery list of
items everyone wants

i started loving mom when we spent sundays looking past
former dad, his gay whip cream, a funny looking sickle,
across the bathroom into the kitchen with chapped hand
towels, and noticing there, a woman: mom

she held tenderly her berry yeast hollow. a deserted filled
donut with jam inside the whole thing gasped

then there's me on top a bunkbed staring at the skys ceiling
mural thinking only of mom. with her burning disco planet
that didn't shine under daylight, the orb came out at
night

3: i didn't go near caves until i understood what
exploring my own shark might mean. rubbing a little purple
ponys head against a blazing mane covered in white hanes.
the spandex belt barely holding hell in place

like a piece of fruit falling out of the fridge pleading for a
hard blade. for any attempt to bareback the forgotten. no one
was able to tell me why i loved this molds peach, this piece
of fuzz clinging to clean tile for girl perspective. the cabinet
drug peddled a normalcy item for resale. our expirations
were read fearful of judgement as loving as the first honey
bloat disarray. *let's 'connect'*

there was a time when transference was pulling seaweed
across shores. shoelaces playing a sink tub wash. moms
clean habits rubbing off on me against the mask of caked
eyeliner this

is an origin story. romantic love a remix of *I heart Mom*. this
brings mummying to a head. mom is bed

4: the idlewild trip outed the womans joint insinuendo, scrambling the transmission of guilts cause in effect. in the stream, a 2for1 intimacy system, she slides her finger across its surface, marveling its creek. her hiking shoes level the sly mugworts, unwilding. she cuts cognition from recognition, throwing the queen out

this is the difference between a caretakers and an undertakers eye. fassbinder leaves us three girls behind. petra, karina, malinger. someone's a man. everything in german is 24 euros plus seconds per minute per. we couldn't afford her for long, stalking me at hot lunch to detail a few boring dreams. she calls my pain arousing, a thick unacknowledged petrified knowledge

die dame is not here for mystery or beauty. between she and me is a rubber hose, thick effect of the jump cut from trip to slip. lisping this morning mom called and makes a request that you not look at her on saturdays. without her unrolled lipstick, she no longer felt her breasts

a horns drive for completion the horse threw itself out the window the woman later moved into the woods they moved the woods

5: she went to the forest to get out of the tree

place is made like this vantage point worn through moths
eaten sweater. she refuses to eat the canned pills mashed.
everyone in town says the sad pinetree monument is a
needle. the opioid tells the bar hostess it's time to grieve. the
faux pas gives us diaper rash. across the room i witness my
girlfriend sink down next to her

one night she dreams the new woman gumming her out,
telling her something she couldn't grow who knew someone
she didn't. she pulls on my strand softly and waits, a lit saint
candle to pray. the drugstore purchase becomes the future
against the other womans slit thesis. i wanted her to know
she isn't here in this log hut with so many fresh snorting
tenderized locks

loose deer turned jerk venison

tiny cabin is a victim scrubbed clean. i no longer think about
her eyebrow stuck perfectly above my lip. the electrical cord
choked itself out

6: she woke from the blackout in the back of the fast
bender. none of them noticed. she tried out her memory
scarefully, scene after scene. pubic details imposed
themselves, the ones she hadn't remembered the first time

she was late to the films and often missed the beginnings, in
this way she could no longer make sense of words, she
stopped listening to the subtitles coming on the screen

through other people she was more likely to talk to herself

how can you shut down if i don't open up?

to a hole the viewers never exactly see

her own story with little or no plot or point, the type of story
no one reported unless a man was making this film, because
everything sounded better inside dad

7: what the director wanted to say eluded translation, a
copy editor inserting his errors. people might be able to read
this cookbook but she was hard to make

it didn't matter if frankfurters were on top or not, the bitch
dialogue was offering up a lesson to learn from this bark

four films (1) dreamed up delusional blonde with amnesiac
hollywood brunette rape (figure 2) american assisting
mountain tits being eyed behind french elder woman bush
(threesome) monotoned mute actress and nurse blended and
orgied cutting glass to match (4) german lesbian spun out
wrung up in a doll with tattered blooms

medusa whirlpools

a character is taken by her elbow, leading to loss of freedom.
she loves her mistress but is tired of watching boredom
screw. they go together to find the scratch to crotch ratio. B
meets her at point 2 and annihilates her there

8: the online thing shows her mom the photos who
says she's a girl who exploits cold nipples, eye-fucks, keeps
pining. there's marlene dressed as humorless white goddess,
barebacklit

she no longer goes into the establishing shot where she gets
to keep living an organs stained rug. she separates from the
audience, no longer subdominant. she keeps thinking about
the other woman and the new woman, no sense of frame
continuity. the outfit is too tight

she lives in a slavetower, an engorged room, naked lady
mannequins, a single shag carpet. its stiff fiberssense
elliptical fiction misting over another pets cemetery. the bra
sadist constricting everyones interlocking tits to keep object
relations in check, a ravens talons

the power cord slinks into the room to backlight sex work.
hopes for the best and makes her instant coffee night until it
hates her. there's a master by the headcase, the subject line
decides

she is my mister, my hairbrush, my panty liner or itch or
obstruction. i eat her stakes. tines pierce eating disorders as
mom says to watch out for girls you wouldn't trust to light
your cigarette

9: home dog stomachs a new noodle fetishist, feeding
her too much too fast too dark in the films theater to read
about it on a phone. she hasn't yet bottomed out but her
body has been sloping at the aisles, breaking off her nails
just to remember what failure looks like

landing in the new womans eyelashes

later on the back of the ticket stub, she is the manager and
oversees a sequence of pictures she can't quite describe her
head researcher says

> *multiples condition the experience of place*
> *so pain ends with gratitude for the damage*
> *that created 'you'*

each time we take a staircase under the floor

10: maria in the clouds plays better than betty as diane
as camilla while ingesting her personal assistant valentine. a
larger bursting of naomi is what's needed straight at kristen
stewarding primal scream the film is a lot less homo than the
trailer makes us want for

her peaks or her grace are like those girls who fail to control
the signal, reenactment being a lame poison for the cure. i
think she's from down under somewhere

either way camillas threats are the realness thing. anyway
that's what rita says. her bad jerking off a pagan roadblock
nipple confidence

between being somebody and having a body

the fact that you're not here

an oracle to satan

the dead woman living with her in the apartment

11: back in fact my coffees shop owner asks me to
yelp

her nametag frowns out like the wrinkles skinning hot cocoa

i want to feel the pin in her shirt it's the only way my fingers

will stop breaking tips from trying. the pine table belongs to
a former tree that can't contain it. the silence gets me off as
repeating what someone says back to them implies customer
feedback. i leave a comment card

the other character sits on my burial ground and no one is
allowed to live there but her. the lungwort realtor sells me
magical rags to wipe clean remnants of sad head. i am
surrounded by these speechless dolls

a spell projecting the new woman onto the ceiling wakes
me. an impasse through a doorjamb: the framed portrait of a
termite staring back

12: a dream where sharing is becoming

her fear about bed death turns out to be correct. changing
partners was a lodging sign along the betrayed mental
patients highway between A cup and a long delicious
intestine. sometimes a shovel behaves as though it has a
consciousness all its own. the cop insists it's a brooms
function to be swept and buried alive

this space isn't hers. there is a chop block for pieces to be
filtered into the center. all the women in the theater think
they're overweight, too small and not enough mercury for
this pilgrim. faulty rhythms created from a movie twins
belief in the split screen being one screen entire. and
becoming what is happening in the specific cutoff part. *no i
can and i will* the new woman said to her therapist, who was
playing her

Thirst Section

[in wood country we liked to wake up at noon]

in wood country we liked to wake up at noon in a leisurely way
making up Theorys of adult relationships, motivated by jealousy as
aromatherapy. lavender replaced leather. everyone was over their
dom for old times stake. i volunteered to separate the cockroaches
into groupings of scare culture and fake meat, our fear of the
anima and insects making it easy to enjoy the broad scope of flavor
profiles taken from palms. the odors came from equipment

this afternoon i woke up burning my face on a sadistic oversize
sofa, not knowing the location of my crumb muffin. the lukewarm
milk froth got flatter as it contemplated reducing itself to a We
Need. *look into the mirror* she said onto the mirror. this was a tourist
attraction

apparently these women were all related which is what i learned
when i went into the bathroom to take a picture of my stomach

> we are starving to crop up
> like pieces of dust caught on the rim
> to prove a brief bio of each You

we hunted

[how many ghouls in her are oppressed]

how many ghouls in her are oppressed sources of resentment?
linens climb into bed to hide. at home my new girlfriend binds
herself to a sad telephone. i ask for her name but the machine
doesn't answer

> no memory of no
> consistency from a deeper cause
> can't know its tendencies

later, her lips stuck to a sugary rim at a mountain dive bar, her
eyes left themselves to some other town. near the fireplace the
taxidermy deer offers 50 cents for her cheap sunglasses, signaling
how many years left she has to be unhappy

across the bar the olive relaxed its pimento into alcohol and was
impressed to the tooth. we found the lounging chair a dealer,
stuffing her deck. the painkilling sadness game was continued in
some fashion until all cards played the winning hand named jack.
loved ones get in his way in the walls of the restrooms 40 mirrors

> substitute spine teacher
> women of a certain age
> angry teenagers
> roaming murders of crows
> a screaming earth
> zen playmix, i ask
> my former houseguest to lie down and die

[myopia was our utopia since]

myopia was our utopia since we were no one interspersed with
subservient communes that functioned like commas, punctuating
our lust chalet with rising waters. the vodka served tater tots,
the fireplace hood ornament a reminder of the death of folk. you
ordered ice cubes to chew-drown out the noise. the golden milk
fondled me

      kindling wormwood through the screen
      an outside ally will come into my ear
      no body was just one anymore
      the greasy menu got up delaminated
      itself in the pyre

the fierce heart jumps you back to the elements. not like the mass
market, no date, an expiration without sweet teeth full of dirt. i
can't stop thinking about naomis masturbation, kristins vomit
mountains, all the beads in petras sports bra. the dry forest air
headache ate away

      skin and landscape in a trance
      when laid together
      the broken screen

[i can't remember when my wine]

i can't remember when my wineglass became conscious, screaming
into its own video. petra plugged in the phone to start a stilettos
sense of pleasure drives between you and me, between the shoe
fetish and the lumpen gaze, all class, even whips. resonances dis-
covered in the jumps between posting about it and telling you how
i feel

room temperature smells and newspaper scraps collided. time
zoned out, a conversation involving activated grass. cocks roached,
the

> wildwood faces compare me
> but won't leave me alone

i am never invited. smoked bears filling my holes, i end up buried in
honey as the bee dies in its glass

> craving only a feeling
> will hold you
> now if you are sick i
> am not two

climate changed. girl children showed up hungry and confused by
unedited foreign

> desire without a trained ear
> arms like battlefields
> our flat feet stepping
> i really did love

[what is difference if we're all living]

what is difference if we're all living in the same apartment

the dreambodies hero makes her way

past a fish crying for help

the ego is not a self-sustaining system. the tuna stalkings girl was
a dancer made of organs, bearing messages about a former dom.
my body has known many of them, this one was special. the lie was
the private part. all language gets her alterations in secret, women
opening oneself to rescue

i jump out of bed aware that i am suspended above skinless beings.
i hear the new young grass blanketing the outside, waiting. there
are so many bushes coming out of the drought. the gold chain is
forgetting bondage

> so many objects of protection
> words of power won't need

i wanted to know it all better and more. to become one open-
minded cunt

[on the class room the visiting artist]

on the class room the visiting artist in the program says that
another woman is still boning my head until I learn to jam a knife.
it was an old institution and cuando necesitas was hung from the
ceiling asbestos in balance. every series lecture was a continuous
erection of thought said our grease leader. the pdfs i was offered
told me newfound health had become illness, re-oppressing the
beautiful. all country girls needed to counter their sad unripe man-
gos. no longer a peach, they were barren rotten on one side

[my girlfriend and i inhabit a loft]

my girlfriend and i inhabit a loft gay dwelling for one. a yellow
faded globe lives bedside, the folding table elevates a hairbrained
plant. the former guests note: this sad agave senses everything with
its atmosphere pricks. labor of the windswept palm outside mirrors
a lizards afterlife. it watches waiting for me to add powdered milk
to instant grounds and begins to inhabit me like my former mis-
tress. smog enters the room and i wait for it to arrive in my laptop
and tell me to make money. the el greco sky is amazing. i witness
my new friends pan dulce harden like concrete. breadcrumbs invite
all the ants crying out for help in their autonomous bodies. it was in
this place that feelings began

[in this new country every old acronym]

in this new country every old acronym is quickly replaced by a
pseudo name (sic). everyone is someones else. she goes to the largest
church to spray incense knees bent eyelids down as she enters the
baroque. god nuts into the earth, gray particles filling her lungs:
undead. that's why she couldn't leave her head, she had a hack of
death. in the shrine coke cans open onto an altar. the teddy bear is
a saint who suffers its brown fur. rosary beads count themselves
lucky martyred against a tree

> the mary candle doubles into my socket
> gothic pop nostalgia appears
> on this page eaten by acid
> the child by the cracked column
> documents her feelings as
> the organ pipes

[as the streets walk me my mother figure]

as the streets walk me my mother figure texts *i owe that beautiful
bitch a voice memo.* afterwards i eat with a student of man. he stops
to finger our server. the menus face has a famous unibrow. a skulls
mask is watching on every rose wall. the tortillas plead to rise
again. fake marigolds droop, communing with their nature. in the
same restaurant across the street, we were told the meat had died
recently

i didn't even need to speak

       words were an underworld
       in incoherent folds
       she was a guidebook but had lost her mother
       i wanted to help find her

[back in language school a spirit]

back in language school a spirit flashlight was the food holes sucked
the most, translated. youtube head fractals were snorted uncut. the
inhale of a dissociative life harmonized hidden parts. on the way
back from rome somehow my mustache driver asked me where
i was going from and then *this radio track is as smooth as a dolphin
vagina*

the dream industrial complex is stuck in everyones mouth

the other gender artists begged for analysis from supportive wire
bras, to allay an itchy moistness bucking tensions

       i am representation

       sweetnothing mask

       spermicide

       a dry region/rainy season

       a midwifes appetite

[the footstools were all hard femme, all]

the footstools were all hard femme, all sinew, and they were good
at their sturdy thought. they wore straitjackets of classic black and
boning corsetry but i had my own foothold

that's their symptom. that's what was happening. all around us
were high towers and inside was a pinball machines arcade project.
i could never remember how to play flaneur. i had lost my token

the coyote came to be my friend and i had a video taken with us
together. we held our heads close to one another to play animal. the
building camera who shot us was sheathed in masochism, a tongue
taste for flagellomania. this was the sum of fasting saints and
highbrows who wore lace boyshorts. i was no longer anyones power
button. i skipped the bit about spinning. i skimped the bits on the
too soft mattress, still serving nature by tying to work against her
risk management problem

[only my sideshow soul manager]

only my sideshow soul manager cares, the one to whom thorny
answers matter. i hunt a driver to take me beaten to a new path. he
gives no ratings to this urn. i can't blame him. the sea level rises to
wash away our borders

up the cobbled streets we see the public private complex depicting
upright cactus colors in vain. *what are we?* asks my relationship
in this walled-only space, this hell designed by an architexts help
guide. these paper mask survivors belong to the body but can't hold
it without paying. this is the brands progress. this is how pain turns
to paying. this is loves grabbing chokehold

[but she did have one ritual]

but she did have one ritual: undressing. she moistened the iguanas
skin daily, preparing for the appearance of self. she dipped her
brush in still life watermelon. appetites envisioned more than
she could. instead of traveling she read travel books, played drag
king to hurt feminine pride: a coffins best kept secret remains the
painkillers

        2 fridas meet in the jungle
        strangled in the neck of the woods
        through a divorce
        'my nanny and i' (fig. 1)
        (the figure is hurting herself)

        paid out traces
        to lubricate dark matter
        plays in the doll house
        stutter at her pink thong
        with its own echo

        two nudes in this jungle
        passions pain palimpsest
        she is and isn't (sick)
        stretched out on a green billiard table
        the other constellation

[she scraped in a frustrated way, freedom]

she scraped in a frustrated way, freedom unsatiated by. premature
capitulation does not exist in a vacuum. she lived to arrange the
bones side by side in the closet tomboys house, a wetnurse

here the vanishing point fingers herself. the clouds in the sky
juxtapose brows and the ruched skirt below. my mother says
beauty exists despite the drought. because we're in the suburbs
where everyone likes to feel like an object pushed into presence.
my girlfriend hates that i give without words through an amateurs
technique of stroking, daubs of being. it was and is still somewhere
in the past. this morning? years ago? a decision has been made to
proceed with the day. so i do

    threading is a real thing. why is a knot

no one can the New Woman says

[back in Death valley, in former]

back in Death valley, in former sub country, she brushes to stroke
blank when painting the desert sublime. but she doesn't want to
move the chains of chance. she doesn't want color detached from
substance, she wants to be as factual as possible but also to bristle
areas of wet sensation. to grab a tube and squeeze, to throw up
paint. so the broken easel went inside

the dog shit on the celebritys fake lawn proved to us death was real.
it was better than a man on his dogma. i had begun to fall for the
hard quiet of the animal in everything plastic pointing straight
to heaven. hard tips mirroring contours of muscle. even pecs flex
against the harness. dry grass had given up a cakes touch

we all walked toward the earth with moisture to spare. she felt a
critical distance from it because Dad had become a business reply, a
noname.doc, and girlhood a pink swan float navigating

the shallow pool contains two dimensional figures, one over stand-
ing, one boy under pants. the cancellation of a cancellation

every david is about two people: the artist and the drowning
subject. solitudes separated by bad choices, soggy hosts, goals
encrusted in chested manscapes. the linen jacket flew all the way
from Kensington. dad left like this though he held the stud long
enough but mom knew she couldn't be in the castle with so many
shaved princes

cretin, creatinine, scrotal adrenal axis fuchsia in situ

a horizontal crime divides the canvas into a bottom geometry and
a soiled top. various skids mark the oblique, dividing the body up

by taking myriad shots at it, then reassembling and going back for
seconds and when using a memory collage method lingering along
the blunt

imaging the thing makes the thing. preposthumously at that
moment I wanted her to be there too. when we meet again the smell
of our melting lashes will be so pungent it will beg us to

dad taught me diving straight. once again this cremated painting
proves it, symbolizing his interior hockneyed goliaths former david.
after what one was is taken away what is one? lines delay the future.
prime rib and two veg. a turtlenecks black hole pulls us into each
others

Acknowledgments and Notes

Endless gratitude to these people who kept me going during the writing of this book: Nicholas Muellner, Mariel Williams, Céline Kuklowsky, Julie Moon, Micki Davis, Mark Gindi, Danielle and Jameel Haque, Daniel K, my sister, and my parents. There are many, many others.

This book would not be possible without Mark Levine. I am forever grateful.

Thank you to the University of Iowa Press for all. Thank you to the *Columbia Review* for publishing excerpts.

The first line of the stanza on page 21 is inspired by imagery from Donna Stonecipher's "The Ruins of Nostalgia 7."

The last lines of 26 borrow language from Jennifer L. Knox's "Ballet on the Radio."

Kuhl House Poets

Christopher Bolin
Ascension Theory

Christopher Bolin
Form from Form

Shane Book
Congotronic

Oni Buchanan
Must a Violence

Oni Buchanan
Time Being

Michele Glazer
On Tact, & the Made Up World

David Micah Greenberg
Planned Solstice

Jeff Griffin
Lost and

John Isles
Ark

John Isles
Inverse Sky